Of Leaves & Ashes

Patty Ho
何世嫻

OF LEAVES & ASHES by Patty Ho (何世嫻) is a collection of poems: among these, some relate to philosophy and some to old Chinese poems to which Patty Ho has added new thoughts. Others are more musical and are additionally presented on the accompanying CD as songs.

Love and pain, dreams and disillusion, leaves and memories, ashes and hopes, encounters and homecomings, sorrow and beauty... all are interwoven in the poems in this book.

The notes contain Patty Ho's translations of the Chinese poems quoted in the book.

Patty Ho has an intense interest in English and Chinese poetry, philosophy and music. She found inspiration for her poems from the enlightening thoughts of great philosophers as well as from the poetry of the Tang and Sung Dynasties. This book integrates treasured quotations and inspiration from famous philosophers and poets (both Chinese and Western) across the centuries.

The essay 'A solitary song for nothing', which concludes the book, discusses poetry and philosophy.

The CD accompanying the book consists of poems and songs written and sung by Patty Ho to music composed by herself. Most of the songs are in English, but two of the old Chinese poems are sung in Cantonese; another song is sung half in Putonghua and half in English.

Philosophy, poetry, music and songs, concerning existence, truth, love and beauty, are intermingled in this book of leaves and ashes...

PATTY HO (何世嫻) was born in Hong Kong. She studied law in the University of Hong Kong and is now practising as a solicitor in a local law firm. She studied philosophy in the Master of Arts in Philosophy (part-time) programme at the Chinese University of Hong Kong. She is also interested in singing and writing music for poems.

Apart from her interest in philosophy and music, she has always been a poetry lover and poetry still remains what she loves most. She first started to write poems in her secondary school days, in Form Six, and has kept up her interest in reading and writing poems ever since.

Time and experiences in life have deepened her love for poetry, and the study of philosophy has given her inspiration for writing some deeper and thought-provoking poems. Apart from words, she loves to express her poetry in music and songs. What she strives to attain is to unfold the pages of her poems, pour out her songs and stars, transform sorrow into beauty, and paint her own essence with love.

Of Leaves & Ashes

Patty Ho
何世嫻

Proverse Hong Kong

Of Leaves & Ashes
by Patty Ho.
1st paperback edition published in Hong Kong
by Proverse Hong Kong, May 2016.
Copyright © Proverse Hong Kong, May 2016.
ISBN:978-988-8228-04-1

1st published in multimedia format in Hong Kong
by Proverse Hong Kong, 19 April 2016.
Multimedia ISBN: 978-988-8228-05-8
Copyright © Proverse Hong Kong, 19 April 2016.

Distribution and other enquiries to:
Proverse Hong Kong, P.O. Box 259, Tung Chung Post Office, Tung
Chung, Lantau Island, NT, Hong Kong SAR, China.
E-mail: proverse@netvigator.com
Web: www.proversepublishing.com

Page design by Proverse Hong Kong.
Cover image by and with kind permission of Annie Ho (何世琪).

British Library Cataloguing in Publication Data.
A catalogue record for this book is available
from the British Library.

無數的你

在這裏，沒有華麗浮誇的詞藻
在這裏，沒有艱澀堆砌的思想
在這裏，沒有暴力的磚頭

在這裏，有不再沉默的風景在歌唱
在這裏，有 "死可以生"[1] 的情在起舞
在這裏，哲學與詩歌交融，音樂和美流溢，蝶與夢齊飛

風，依舊是那風
風吹葉落，化為裊裊不死之灰
人間滄桑
你，是否依然是你？
無數的你微笑
在春天裏

親愛的讀者，請容許我一同邀請您，"溯游從之"[2]。

蒹葭
2-2016

Countless You

Here, there are no splendid exaggerated words.
Here, there are no difficult piled up thoughts.
Here, there are no bricks of violence.

Here, scenes that cannot be silenced are singing;
Here, love that can raise the dead is dancing;
Here, there is blending of philosophy and poetry;
Music flows with beauty; butterflies soar with dreams...

Wind, still that wind.
Wind blows, leaves fall, turning into undying ashes that rise;
The vicissitudes of life
You, are you still you?
Countless you smiling
In Spring

Dear readers, may I invite you to sail down the stream in search
of the leaves and ashes...

"Reeds"
February, 2016
Translated by Patty Ho

A Shared Journey of Discovery

Patty is an emotionally sensitive lady.

She loves to write. She loves to sing. She writes and sings with her heart.

Patty writes mostly lyric poems. To quote Milton's description of poetry in his tractate "On Education" (1644), her poems are "simple, sensuous and passionate".[3]

I came to know Patty when we studied philosophy together a number of years ago. I did not, however, know her well at that time. Fate had it that a few years later, by sheer chance we rekindled a friendship that had slipped past us. We met very rarely, but we wrote to each other from time to time. We exchanged thoughts on a wide range of topics: philosophy, history, art, and the idiosyncrasies of life.

Amongst the topics that Patty liked to reflect upon was love and death. I like Rainer Rilke. She too.[4] So we talked a lot about Rilke and Marina Tsveteva and shared many anecdotes of the two. We shared our thoughts on the works and stories of many other poets too – from the tragic death of Gu Cheng (顧城) to Emily Dickinson's haunting poem 'Ample make this bed'; from the touching "nameless poems" of Li shang-yin (李商隱) to the colorful life of the beautiful Japanese poetess Ono no Komachi (小野小町) – Patty's love of poetry and resourcefulness impressed me a lot. I told her about the story of the brief (but emotionally lasting) encounter between Isaiah Berlin and the Russian poetess Anna Akhmatova, and the poem that she wrote ('Cinque') after their meeting. Patty was very moved when she read the following lines:

And that door that you half opened,
I don't have the strength to slam.
It was then that I found out that Patty was a very

emotionally sensitive person.

"A poet is, before anything else, a person who is passionately in love with language", said Auden.[5] Patty is a lover of language. In one of her emails to me, she expressed agreement with the view that language was more than just a tool of communication: "Language tickles, sprinkles and sparkles... it tickles our feelings, sprinkles our mind, and sparkles our imagination". A well-written poem, as former American poet laureate Rita Dove puts it, "should haunt you a little. Or, let's just say, it should accompany you".[6]

Patty loves music too. She likes to compose music for her own poems. Music is naturally a good friend of poetry. Both are embedded with sound and rhythm. Even when we read a poem silently to ourselves, the poem makes a pleasant sound to the ear of the heart. This is perhaps why, in the days of the Greeks, poems were invariably sung as an aural art.

Patty loves to sing out her poems. In this book readers will have the opportunity of listening to her singing. She may not be the best singer in the world, but she puts her soul into what she sings. It is always pleasing to discover how she marries poetry and music together.

Despite their natural affinity, poems are of course different from music. Poems are made of words and words carry conceptual meaning that is distinctly different from what may sometimes be called the "meaning of music". Poems are subject to interpretation in a way different from music. In every poem that Patty writes, one finds a persona behind it that speaks the story of the poetess, her feelings and her mind. A fleeting moment of emotion that she seized upon, a perspective that suddenly dawned upon her, an episode of day-dreaming that stole her heart – she penned these into her poems and transformed them into an eternal stream of consciousness that is re-lived every time her poems are read by a reader.

It may be said that when a poem is written, it takes on a life of its own. Every reader interprets the poem in their own way, against their own experiences, and in the context of their own being. The reader freely appropriates the author's consciousness as his or her own, and finds new meaning to it that might never have been contemplated by the author. Yet the persona behind the poem is always there. She leads the reader – by the words that she writes – to make his own investigation. It is, in truth, a shared journey of discovery.

Patty once shared her thoughts on poetry with a few of her "philosophy friends" in a presentation which she titled 'A Solitary Song of Nothing'. She talked about the solitariness of a poetess, whose feelings and emotions were laid bare before her readers whenever she published her poems – the paradox of solitariness on public display. I would, however, view the paradox in a slightly different way. Poetry, in my view, is a joint venture between the poetess and her readers. Drawn together by the calls of their being, the poetess and her readers are engaged in a journey: a shared journey of discovery.

Horace Wong
January 2016

A Rare Combination...

Referring to Hölderlin, Heidegger speaks of poetry as "like a dream, and not reality; a playing with words, and not the seriousness of action. Poetry is harmless and ineffectual."[7] This however is not the true nature of poetry. Indeed, poetry is not philosophy. It does not explain or analyze reality. It describes, uncovers the phenomenon with words, so that we have a different awareness of the world, a colourful and sentimental feeling with what we encounter in our everyday life-world. We are guided by the lyrical words which are engendered by the sensitivity of the poet. Through these lines, we are transposed to a different world. We see and feel differently.

The poetry of Patty leads us to see and feel differently. There is a rare combination of philosophy, especially the classical Greek and contemporary European philosophy, with traditional Chinese literature. Her poetry shows us the world of thinking and feeling, love and tragedy, sadness and happiness, peace and turmoil, memory and oblivion, desire and frustration, and truth and untruth.

This is not easy reading. We have to open our heart and let the poetic words fill up our mind. Then we can share the joy and the dream with Patty of uncovering the truth of the experience of our lives. Then we gain new insight and inspiration from things neglected by us in our busy everyday life.

Professor Cheung Chan-Fai
February, 2016

Author's Introduction and Acknowledgements

Readers may like to know why I have entitled this book, "Of Leaves & Ashes". – Leaves carry thoughts and memories of trees, and ashes return to earth from which new trees and leaves may grow. Poems carry thoughts and memories of the poet who may be regarded as "dead" when his/her poem is finished and they then become open to the interpretation of different readers, and may in turn lead to new thoughts and hopes.

The painting on the front cover of *Leaves & Ashes* is by my sister Annie. She told me that the shapes of the twirling leaves coming down were done with dried leaves from her garden, dipped in paint. In her painting, although ashes lie black on the ground, the use of green shows that new life is coming. Dancing specks of gold rise up from the ashes. I think that Annie's painting is a wonderful image for the title of my book.

There are three types of poems in this book. Some were written when I was studying philosophy in the Master of Arts in Philosophy (part-time) programme in the Chinese University of Hong Kong and they were inspired by the thoughts of a number of philosophers as learnt from the lectures. Some of the poems are more rhythmical and musical, and, after writing them as poems, I composed music for them and made them into songs as well. Other poems are related to some old Chinese poems which I love and to which I had added some new thoughts. I have also translated them and the translations are given in the notes at the end of the book. When I received a grant from Hong Kong Arts Development Council for my first poetry book, *Heart to Heart*, in 2009, I received a 'Recommendation' by Professor Michael Anthony Ingham. When I re-read the 'Recommendation' five years later, I was amazed to find that the three points mentioned there about my poems – "poetic philosophy", "musicality" and "Chinese poetics" – correspond exactly with the different types of poem in this my second poetry book.

One special feature of this book is the accompanying CD containing videos of poems and songs. Poetry is the music of the soul and poetic language has a kind of musicality in itself. Sometimes after writing or reading a poem, I love to compose a melody for it and sing it out. Since the publication of my first poetry book, I have been dreaming of making a CD of songs for my poems. In order to realize my dream, I spent much time and considerable effort in writing the melodies, taking music lessons from Mr Henry Poon, taking singing lessons from Dr Ezra Chan, and going through all the practising, recording and editing of the songs. I am very fortunate to have these two good teachers who have given me so much help, support and encouragement. I know that I am not a good singer and might have asked another person to sing the songs in the CD for me. But I wanted to sing those poems which I wrote myself and hope that those who listen to them will excuse my poor singing.

Some poems in this book were inspired by images and these are shown in the CD. They are, 'To Part', 'Golden Shower', 'Of walnuts and almonds', 'Two Solitudes', 'The Gaze', and 'Side by Side'. The poem 'Home of Bitterness' was inspired by the painting '苦瓜家園' by Wu Guanzhong.

My father was the founder of "Taiyar Books Company" (大雅圖書公司), and as a child I used to be a model posing for the pictures in his books. The name "Taiyar" (大雅) means "elegant writings" and comes from the Book of Odes or Shijing (詩經) which is the oldest existing collection of Chinese poetry. The poems 'Of walnuts and almonds' and 'Of cakes and women' in this poetry book are especially dedicated to my late parents, and the video in Track No. 19 of the accompanying CD shows a picture taken from a page in one of the Taiyar books written by my father.

There have been a lot of things to learn and many hurdles to overcome before this book together with the CD could finally be completed. I would like to thank my teachers, Henry Poon and Ezra Chan, my sister Annie for the book cover image, Professor Cheung Chan Fai for his Preface, Horace Wong, S.C., for his essay, 'A Shared Journey of Discovery', "Reeds" for his Chinese poem, 無數的你 ('Countless You'), Timothy Yuen who gave permission to use the picture from a Taiyar book mentioned above in the CD, The Reverend Nicholas Cooper who read the opening and closing announcements in the CD, Dr Gillian Bickley who assisted me in preparing this book for publication, and all those who have inspired or in any way supported my poetry.

Patty Ho (何世嫻)

Of Leaves & Ashes by Patty Ho 何世嫻

III Of Leaves and Ashes

IV A Solitary Path

Prior Publication Acknowledgements

The following poems appeared in Patty Ho, *Heart to Heart* (Proverse 2010) 'Serenade',' Miss you'. The following poems and accompanying images also appeared in *Heart to Heart*: 'Fragments', 'Nocturne', 'To Part'. All appear here courtesy of the publishers, Proverse Hong Kong. The following poems appeared in a booklet published by the Philosophy Department of the Chinese University of Hong Kong: 'Without Why', 'O Possibility!', and 'Words'.

Illustration credits

All illustrations in the CD are by Patty Ho with the following exceptions: illustrations for 'Fragments' and 'Nocturne', by Annie Ho; 'Flowers like snow', by Simon Tu; 'Of walnuts and almonds', as published by Taiyar publishers; 'Of cakes and women', childhood photo taken either by Patty Ho's father or her uncle; 'Everything and Nothing', detail from *The Birth of Venus* (1879) by William-Adolphe Bouguereau, Musée d'Orsay. The reproduction of *The Birth of Venus*, from which the detail is taken, is a faithful reproduction of a two-dimensional public domain work of art and is therefore in the public domain. The photographic reproduction is therefore also considered to be in the public domain in the United States.

I

When poetry and philosophy meet

"When the world has long forgotten you,
  to the silent earth say: I am flowing.
  To the rushing waters speak: I am!"[8]
      – *Rainer Maria Rilke*

Without Why

"The rose is without why, it blooms because it blooms.
It pays no attention to itself, asks not whether it is seen." [9]
   – Angelus Silesius

Don't ask, don't ask
why the rose blooms.
It blooms, it blooms
because it blooms.
Let us step back
and let life disclose
its mysteries to us.

Don't ask, don't ask
why I love you.
Let me, let me
show you my love.
We come close and drift apart
in the eternal cycle
of Love and Strife. [10]

Along the path of life
we search high and low.
What will we find
and what will we lose?
Don't we know this ordered universe
was, is and shall be ever-living Fire,
kindled and quenched in measure? [11]

Don't ask, don't ask.
Let Being itself
unfold the answer to us.

O Possibility!

"Higher than actuality stands possibility."[12]
        – *Martin Heidegger*

O possibility!
Where are you?
Lurking in the shadows
or dancing in my dreams?
Are you yes or are you no?
Fulfillment or disillusion?

So many times, I lose myself
in the midst of the They;
yet you show me the way
to choose my authentic self,
to write my own poem of life.

Elusive and luring,
indefinite and daring,
you lead me on and on
to pursue the music of my dream,
to reach the place where I can be.

Though thrown into being without choice,
before the most certain possibility comes,
I am still possible
to make my existence
beautiful and authentic.

Pure Intuition

" ...it is the phenomenological theory of essence alone
that is capable of providing a foundation for a philosophy
of the spirit."[13]
    – *Edmund Husserl*

How I love to watch
the stars in the sky
and think of those in your eyes,
the passion shining from your soul.

How I love to find
the moon in the dark
and search for that in your heart,
the pure you inside the worldly you.

May you also see me
with your inner eye
to find the pure I
and music of my soul,
bracketing all mundane views,
my looks, status, whatever.

Let's not take for granted
anything conventional
but seek the true beginning
to grasp the essence and meaning.
Let philosophy mingle with poetry
to play a song of truth, love and beauty.

Words

"...whenever we exchange words with one another, we
share the world."[14]
> – *Hans-Georg Gadamer*

What I want
isn't a bouquet of flowers
but a bouquet of writings.
Flowers bloom; flowers fade.
Words stand; words stay.
Something they say,
some truth they unconceal,
if only we care to hear
and let them be a bridge
not a barrier between hearts.

Are they truth or untruth?
Do they disclose or hide
the true feelings in the heart?
Will they bring us to the Open
where the light of beauty shines?
In the circle we move round and round
with understanding only partial;[15]
meanings open and close
in the enigma of the game.

Everything and Nothing

"It is a play of traces or différance
that has no sense and is not,
a play that does not belong."[16]
  – Jacques Derrida

From you I learn –
the beautiful sorrow
of the foam, the swallow...
everything is nothing
nothing is everything;
a poem should be silent,
strong as stone, light as mist,
its words dance in the breeze,
only to be foamed
in the heart of heart.

A blue swallow flies into my dream,
taking me everywhere and nowhere.
In my mirror Venus rises from the foam,
letting down her long soft hair.
The moon sighs a little;
stars glisten with memories.
Nothing lasts,
everything stays;
traces /trace/ and efface...

Pure and True

"In words we are at home."[17]
        – Hans-Georg Gadamer

Say it pure,
say it true.
Let words soothe,
let words home
our restless hearts
in a shaking world,
things falling apart.

Apple, apple –
we learn, we share,
asking and answering,
taking and giving.
Experience and taste
the sweet, the bitter.

Open to possibilities,
braving cold, hurt,
and disillusionment;
live through each word.
On the solitary path,
venture for the encounter
with the distant Other,
and find the inmost I.

To Time

"Time is a child playing a game of draughts
the kingship is in the hands of a child."[18]
 – *Heraclitus*

Are you "what"
or are you "how"?
Does the answer matter
so long as in you I feel,
I perceive, I love, I live?

Are you a test
for the validity of truth,
the strength of faith,
the power of hope,
the eternity of love?

Where are you?
Behind me, before me,
surrounding me everywhere?
This moment I try to grasp you,
the next moment you are gone.
Oh, how can I make you stay
or rewind to past happy days?

Are you moving like an arrow
forever pointing forward,
or turning like a circle
taking us back to where we start?
Are you the blink of an eye,
or a maya, or just nothing?

On the swing of life we rise and fall,
till the day we are no more
while you play on and on…

The Horizon

"I stand above the world,
which has now become for me,
in a quite peculiar sense, a phenomenon."[19]
       – *Edmund Husserl*

Where are we?
In the mundane world
or transcendental realm?
Deeper and deeper we go
to unearth different layers of ground
in search of the ultimate meaning.
How shall we find the true path
in the enigma of this world?
Is the world just our belief?

Meeting and parting
in the infinite horizon,
what 'I-you-synthesis' have we made?
what truth and essence have we found?
Is love something a priori?
Can it be grasped by reason?
Like a passing phenomenon,
life and love sail away
across the horizon of haze.

To Empedocles[20]

"I am now one of these, an exile from the gods
and a wanderer, having put my trust in raving strife."[21]
        – *Empedocles*

Dear wanderer,
I see your lonesome shadow
standing tall upon the summit,
your heart catching fire.
Below you spread
the unfathomable depths,
the passionate blaze,
the raving Strife…

You smiled and plunged
into the boiling blood,
the bursting flames
of the vortex of Love,
kindling the petals
of your most exquisite rose.
O to merge with infinity,
to fall and rise in eternity!

What freedom, what ecstasy,
to seal your fate
in the ever-living fire,
to let go and embrace
the eternal mysteries
of Love and Strife!

Wandering no more,
into the fire you vanished,
but the flames won't go away;
they keep burning,
burning my wandering leaves…

In the vagueness

"The ambiguity of poetic language answers to the
ambiguity of human life as a whole and therein lies its
unique value."[22]
    – Hans-Georg Gadamer

You said
poems were vague.
Isn't life just as ambiguous,
without why or where?
Can we reason with fate
or explain each feeling we have?
Don't we need some subtlety,
some tender vagueness,
when truth stares us in the face,
so blatant and painful?

The poet is dead,
opening up new possibilities.
Poems don't teach or preach,
neither right nor wrong.
Oh, song of existence[23]
intending nothing,
a draft of wind singing,
pouring forth and holding back,
shaping and reshaping,
breaking and building,
in the vagueness...

苦瓜家園[24] – Home of bitterness

「罪即是罪, 苦即是苦, 我仍是我...
　不可免之罪, 安然當之; 不可免之苦, 安然受之...」[25]
　　　 － 勞思光

Oh, so bitter,
I taste it on my lips,
I feel it, so real, so deep…
in the picture, outside the picture,
endless threads and loads of sorrow
hanging, knotting, intertwining…

There may be
brighter gardens, fairer fields,
to cultivate sweeter fruits,
but none dearer than the bitter soil,
mother of our spirit's growth.

May we sow
seeds of kindness, seeds of love,
not calculating what to reap.
May we bear
inevitable sins, inescapable griefs,
hearts be grateful and wide.

Tears of bitterness break
through the hopeless dark;
the beauty of sorrow shines,
touching hearts, kindling stars…

Let's cry... let's smile...

"When the world has long forgotten you,
to the silent earth say: I am flowing.
To the rushing waters speak: I am!" [26]
— *Rainer Maria Rilke*

They may crush us with harsh words.
They may tread on us like dirt.
They may break promises and go away.
They may misunderstand us again and again.
They may reward our love with pain and cold.
They may treat our passion with apathy and mock.

Let's cry; why hide?
Let our tears like spring water flow,
tender, nourishing and strong;
new songs may pour forth,
fresh buds may grow,
we never know.

Life may be absurd and bring us woes.
Tragedy may befall us and smash our hopes.
Love may be a dream and fade over time;
it is vulnerable and opens heart to hurt.
We may one day lose what we gain.
We may struggle and persist but all in vain.

Let's smile, and rise above our fate,
setting it to our own music.
Push a rock up a mountain,
it rolls down, push it up over and over.[27]
Amid life's absurdity and sorrow,
we can stand tall.

II

I cry, I smile and I sing…

"True singing is a different breath, about nothing…A wind."[28]

— *Rainer Maria Rilke*

Serenade

"And my song too is the song of a lover."[29]
         – Friedrich Nietzsche

Colour my dream
with the brush of your love.
Paint a smile
on the face of my moon.
Gather stars and moonbeams
to weave a necklace for me.

May our hearts sing
with our different voices.
Let them blend in
harmony and rhythm.
Love me please
for love's sake;
don't ask what we may reap.

Let love be a journey,
a never-ending dream,
in search of beauty and harmony;
forever we will fly . . .

Fragments

Summer, sunshine, shower;
through emerald shadows,
from dream to dream we wander.

Beaches, oceans, freedoms;
heart waves dancing and breaking.
Seashells to pick, secrets to keep;
footprints buried in the shifting sand.

Wild sleepless nights—
row a boat across the moon river,
collecting stars to fill our dreams;
desires burning . . . dissolving
in the tender darkness.

Green hearts hanging in the air
grow towards each other
and drift apart;
fragments of memories
falling, lingering and fading.

So softly, so lightly,
between remembrance and forgetting,
the summer passes by . . .

Nocturne

The night is burning
a poem of darkness;
its flames are singing
a song of nothingness.

In vain I search
for the moon in the waters.
Dreams look so real,
yet always beyond my reach.

When thoughts are too heavy,
I will lay them down
on a bed of rose petals
you scatter into my dream.

When words are too weak,
I will fall silent
and surrender my heart
to the embrace of the dark.

Miss you

Miss you
like a bird misses the sky
blue,
like a hill misses the mist
white,
like a star misses the moon
silver.

Miss you
when I open my eyes.
Miss you
when I close my eyes.
Miss you
when the world can't tell me why
we must be so far apart.

To part...

To part is a second meeting
more intense, more loving...
to gaze at a beloved face in the distance
with a longing of the heaviest lightness,
to continue on the backstage of the mind
a blue dream of moonrise tenderness,
to feel in the recesses of the heart
a closeness no distance can part.

The Voyage (A song never sung)

"My child, my sister,
Think of the rapture
Of living together there!
Of loving at will,
Of loving till death,
In the land that is like you!
The misty sunlight
Of those cloudy skies
Has for my spirit the charms,
So mysterious,
Of your treacherous eyes,
Shining brightly through their tears.

There all is order and beauty,
Luxury, peace, and pleasure."[30]
     – Charles Baudelaire

I read a poem;
it took my heart away.
I long to receive
an invitation to the voyage
like one Baudelaire sent
to his child, his sister.

What a tempting dream
to wander with my brother,
to venture into the unknown,
roaming wild and free
in the misty sunlight,
along the dreamy canals
of some foreign lands.

How it lures me
to transgress the threshold,
to discover what lies beyond
those stark black holes
cut across the whitewashed walls.[31]

The most beautiful voyage
may be one never voyaged
which only lives in a poem,
lingers in our imagination,
like a kiss never kissed,
a song never sung.

Will you?

Will you go with me
to gather the fallen leaves?
Getting near a tall tree,
we pick up its dreams
all scattered on the ground
with the sigh of the wind.

Will you stand by me
like a long-lived tree?
When your bark has turned white,
will you still share with me
the stars in your eyes,
the path to the true I?

Come and sit by me
till I have sung to you
all my beautiful poems,
and never let me go
with the leaves in the wind.

Maya

Will the seagull you saw
fly into my dream
and tell me –
what's the colour of the sea
and your heart?

The sea is so misty;
the waves rise and fall,
feeling so lost.
Is everything a maya,
dwelling in emptiness?

La la la la la la
la la la la la
la la la la
la la la la la la la
la la la la

The sea/Love is so changing;
the tides ebb and flow,
feeling no more.
Is everything a maya,
dwelling in emptiness?

A rainy lane

「 撐著油紙傘，獨自
　　彷徨在悠長、悠長
　　又寂寥的雨巷... 」
　　　　– 戴望舒《雨巷》[32]

Walking down a rainy lane
with my silent umbrella,
what joy or sorrow will I find
at the unknown far end?

Dancing in the shadows of dark
with my invisible piano,
I sing my homeless poems
and burn their love for you.

Drifting in this lonely planet,
where do we belong?
This moment we meet;
next moment we part.

Is love, are you, am I,
just a passing phenomenon,
soon to vanish in the hazy horizon
with the irreversible flow of time?

Whispers in the waters

In the sea of words,
we once swam so close –
whispers in the waters,
a pearl dropped,
our small fingers knotted
in the breaking waves.

You blew ripples
so light and soft
that sank my soul
in the deepest whirlpool.
In the twinkling of a star,
you deposited in my heart
fullness and emptiness
enough to last for a lifetime.

Grasping, I lose;
joining, we split –
I, still I, no longer I;
you, still you, no longer you.

III

Of Leaves and Ashes

"You must be ready to burn yourself in your own flame: how could you become new, if you had not first become ashes."[33]

>   – *Friedrich Nietzsche*

A nostalgic zither

「錦瑟無端五十弦，一弦一柱思華年。莊生曉夢迷蝴蝶，望帝春心托杜鵑。

滄海月明珠有淚，藍田日暖玉生煙。此情可待成追憶，只是當時已惘然！」
　　　– 李商隱　《錦瑟》 [34]

Oh, dream of dawn,
why must you leave so soon?
Was I not a happy butterfly
dancing on wings of love?
Oh, heart of Spring,
whom may I entrust you to?
Or shall I bury you beneath
a pile of Autumn leaves?

See how the smoke rises
above the blue field of jade.
May I play a nostalgic song
on my out of tune zither?
But who will care to listen
to my melancholic melody,
falling with tears of pearl
below the watery moon?

Flowerwords

「花非花，霧非霧，夜半來，天明去，
　來如春夢不多時，去似朝雲無覓處。」
　　　　－白居易《花非花》[35]

Lightly, lightly,
they fell in the air.
Deeply, deeply,
they sank into my dream.

Smile, smile,
flower in the mirror,
moon in the waters,
while stars still shine,
while poems still rhyme.

Sublime, sublime,
ashes of nothingness,
when eternity can't hold,
when love has flown…

Boat of Sorrow

「風住塵香花已盡，日晚倦梳頭。
　物是人非事事休，欲語淚先流。
　聞說雙溪春尚好，也擬泛輕舟。
　只恐雙溪舴艋舟，載不動，許多愁。」
　　　－李清照《武陵春》[36]

Clouds so light...
Sorrow so heavy...
Shall we row the boat of sorrow
across the sea of sailing clouds?
When lightness and heaviness meet,
will clouds carry sorrow away
or, overburdened by grief,
turn into a rain of tears?

Oh, how we have loved
from earth to heaven,
climbing up the ladder of love.
Now coming to the end
of love's path of no return,
shall we leap from the cloud's top,
and transform our many sorrows
into beautiful cloudflowers?

When clouds of eternal love
can no more bear the boat of sorrow,
a million rows of tears alone I weep,
a billion cups of grief aloof I drink.

Greensleeves

「青青子衿,悠悠我心。縱我不往,子寧不嗣音?
　青青子佩,悠悠我思。縱我不往,子寧不來? 」
　　　－《詩經·鄭風·子衿》[37]

On your green green swing,
my heart blithely danced
like the breeze of Spring,
smiling and carefree.

On your soft soft grass,
I spread my tender dream,
waiting for the summer rain,
passionate and sweet.

In your deep deep forest,
I gathered the autumn leaves
to write my homeless poems
and blew them to the wind.

In your cold cold mountain,
I embraced the wintry silence
and burnt my empty songs
in the fire of the snow.

Empty and Full

「去年今日此門中，人面桃花相映紅。
　人面不知何處去，桃花依舊笑春風。」
　　　－　崔護_《題都城南莊》[38]

A bench in the garden,
his breeze, her flower,
once so close: a lovely picture.
Now only an empty space
full of the presence of absence.

The swallows left, only a leaf
singing on the lonely tree
to the silent empty bench,
and shadows everywhere.

The rosy flames die away
after the sparkling encounter
in this full and empty world
where smiles and sighs play
across the bustle and solitude of life.

Golden Shower

「落紅不是無情物，化作春泥更護花。」
　　– 龔自珍《己亥雜詩》[39]

What delight what surprise,
clusters of golden stars
shower upon my soul,
filling it with sunshine smiles,
and melodious dreams anew.

What tenderness what strength,
flowers surrender to the wind;
little yellow butterflies fly,
spreading their wings wide,
dancing the last waltz of life.

What sorrow what beauty,
a yellow carpet of petals lies
on the bosom of mother earth;
love slumbers on in silence,
to rise high and bloom again.

Yesterday

「故人入我夢，明我長相憶。」
－杜甫《夢李白二首》(其一)[40]

It was one of those familiar dreams
floating to visit me when nights were deep;
but each time the feelings were still intense,
as real as if she were right before my eyes,
wearing the same breeze of yesterday.

In one dream I was crying terribly,
begging to know why she had to go,
only to wake up in the middle of the night
to find still wet tears on my face;
in another I was leaping around a house
like a child mad with inexpressible joy
for her coming near and befriending me.

Perhaps she had left
so that in my dreams she may
forever come and stay.
In the abyss of dreams,
I met the former she and I
and the phantasm of
yesterday...

To my dear poetess[41]

「人成各，今非昨，病魂常似秋千索。
角聲寒，夜闌珊。怕人尋問，咽淚妝歡。瞞！瞞！
瞞！」
     – 唐琬 《釵頭鳳》[42]

Time is cruel.
Fate plays; hearts change.
What's close or distant?
What's real or unreal?
The world looks absurdly strange.
In the dark weep alone;
don't yearn for anyone
to come near to dry your tears.
Double sadness this will make.

As lightning strikes
and heaven turns to hell,
let your beautiful soul grow strong
and sing through the dreadful cold.
On a swing sublimed keep swinging
with changing tones of feelings,
playing a unique symphony
of terror and beauty.

To my dear poet[43]

「棄我去者，昨日之日不可留；
亂我心者，今日之日多煩憂。
... 抽刀斷水水更流，舉杯消愁愁更愁。人生在世不稱
意，明朝散髮弄扁舟。」
　　　　　－李白《宣州謝朓樓餞別校書叔雲》[44]

Will you drift into my dream
when the night breeze moans
and my leaves long to roam?
For you I'll burn a candle
in my secret chamber.

Please stay for a while longer.
Such a long way we have to travel,
taking the wrong paths and turns,
tripping over blocks and stones,
words broken, dreams shattered,
in the absurd journey of life.

Oh, come to me
with your poems and wine.
Let's drink and write
our leaves and rhymes,
and scatter their ashes
to the dancing flames.
See how beautifully they burn
in the elegy of the fire,
igniting hearts and stars.

Waving goodbye to life's woes
and sailing with the moon,
we'll loosen our hair in the wind,
row a mad boat across the waves.

The Promise

「人生若只如初見, 何事秋風悲畫扇?」
　　－納蘭性德《木蘭花令·擬古決絕詞》[45]

Is it a new moon waiting to be full
or the seed of a sweet ripe fruit?
Is it a dream made to be broken
or a flower that opens and withers?

Whatever it is,
so lovely to have someone
willing to give us an eternal promise
we can open our heart to trust.

Oh, please don't give it lightly;
it can touch and soothe
as well as break a heart.

To the Mid-Autumn Moon

「人有悲歡離合，月有陰晴圓缺，此事古難全。
但願人長久，千里共嬋娟。」
  － 蘇東坡《水調歌頭》[46]

Are you far or are you near?
Do you dream? Do you feel?
If in the dark I wait and wait,
if into the sky I gaze and gaze,
will you slip out from the clouds of haze
to kindly offer me a tender glance
and shed your glow over the gloom?

In heaven floating so high,
above all emotions and desires,
can you hear the songs and feel the woes
of human hearts in love and pain?
In a world of defects, regrets and flaws,
how can you be so perfect and pure,
your fullness moving me to tears?

O loveliest lantern of solitude,
forever shining, never forsaking…
If my heart screams, will you hear?
If my soul weeps, will you embrace her
in your steadfast cradle of love?
You wax and wane, and return to full;
but some people, some feelings
leave and never come back again.

Under the Starry Sky

「人生不相見，動如參與商。今夕復何夕，共此燈燭
光。」
　　　　　－杜甫《贈衛八處士》[47]

Which star led us
to the boat of friendship,
sharing our wandering hearts
in the shining night shadows?

Below the moon of nostalgia,
in the blue smoke of memory,
can we call back the dead past
and hold upon nearness so far?

Come wind, come rain, come what may,
Sail on, sail on our rocking boat,
in the stream of life's passing dream
through waves of absurdity and paradox.

While fate brings us side by side,
let's fill our glasses full to the brim
and savour the bittersweet wine
of love, of life, under the starry sky...

If you come...

「春夢秋雲，聚散真容易。」
　　－晏幾道《蝶戀花》 [48]

If you come, if you come,
please come with the music of the wind
as it blows away the grey mist
out of which you will emerge,
take me past stars I miss
and leaves from future skies.

If we part, if we part,
let's part in the music of the heart;
when you turn around
to cast me one last glance,
may the cello tenderly play
a beautiful song of goodbye
with the deep waves of the sea...

Of Leaves and Ashes

「前山極遠碧雲合，清夜一聲白雪微。
欲寄相思千里月，溪邊殘照雨霏霏。」
－杜牧《寄遠》[49]

In a snow white coffin,
shivering I lie;
a tear rolls
down the river of night,
reflecting in the crispy dark
with crystalline bright
the sky of yesterday
where a moon of promise kept
a forever steadfast dream.

In the aching cold,
across the clouds of thoughts,
can you feel my snow falling,
can you hear my soul playing
a shadowy silent piano
of leaves and ashes
from which I'll rise
to greet the rain,
to kiss the pain?

IV A Solitary Path

"...the poem is lonely and *en route*... the poem intends another, needs this other..." [50]

     – Paul Celan

Of walnuts and almonds
Dedicated to my father

My dad said
in writing there was freedom
as long as feelings were sincere.
So I believe; so I practise
heart word after heart word,
pouring and emptying myself
in the music of my soul.

With no voice of an angel
nor talent of a great poet,
I am an ordinary human,
my strength, my weakness.
I break shells of walnuts,
struggling and failing.

Drowning in the wavy ocean,
my song screams and quavers,
bitter and little as almonds,
laden with nothingness,
perchance a leaf drifting
by the window of your heart.

Against odds and absurdities,
still I write, still I sing,
my true heart, my small voice,
imperfect but unique.

Of cakes and women
Dedicated to my mother

I grew up with cakes.
Each birthday mum bought me
a big one, soft and sweet.
Girl or woman,
who doesn't like to be spoilt by
beautiful and delicious treats?
Who won't be lured by
softness like kisses, sweetness like love,
melting lips, touching hearts?

In time we learn
life isn't a sweet cake;
sorrow loves to play with joy.
Strength deep down women need
to support their tender leaves.
Let cakes be enjoyed
heartily and gratefully
and into beautiful strength turned.
Let women love and be loved
strongly, tenderly, beautifully…

Who?

When darkness descends,
who will bring me a stone and feather
as the pillow for my soul?
Who will swing with me to the stars
and fall with me into the same dream?

Whose hands will touch my heartstrings
and play a soft lullaby
to cradle me to sleep?
Whose mouth will whisper in my ear
words unsaid or half-said?

Whose eyes will close my eyes
to slumber with the moon?
Whose heart will dance with mine
and embrace it in eternal time?

Row your boat

"Row, row, row your boat
Gently down the stream,
Merrily, merrily, merrily,
Life is but a dream."[51]

Your indefinite silence,
your obstinate indifference,
pain me more than ever.
If only you could whisper a *Hi*
or *Bye* to break this emptiness.
But does it really matter
when the play was over,
the last word spoken,
the curtains dropped?

Sometimes the thought
of our never meeting again,
rowing the same boat,
crossing the same moon,
spreads a winter over my soul,
and snow starts to fall
into my nursery rhyme,
my once merry dream…

Drop a star please

When nights are long
and the moon has gone,
drop a star please
into my hazy dream,
a star to make me weep
to sprinkle my faded leaves,
a star to bring me sparkles
to rekindle my cold ashes
so they'll rise and dance
in beautiful flames again...

Memories

"You were my death
you I could hold
when everything slipped from me." [52]
    – Paul Celan

My poems are imperfect,
with flaws and regrets,
just like life and love,
just like memories…

Oh, could we help
walking the same steps,
falling into the same dream,
living through the same love and pain?

When the dream is over, love's gone,
when life is drawing to a close,
what have we got but memories,
blissful or sorrowful?

A naked tree facing the snow,
I'll let go and die time after time
with each leaf of memory I shed,
writing my memories to the sky,
and let my heart into music break
drifting between heaven and hell.

You may choose to forget,
you may tease my poems,
but you can't annihilate
memories…

An Easter Poem

"Look around:
see how things all come alive –
By death! Alive!
Speaks true who speaks shadow." [53]
             – *Paul Celan*

In the shadow of a dream,
I bake a piece of cake
filled with pearly starlets
and moon-soft petals;
I break a slice for you
in exchange for a leaf.

Dream ends
before the last goodbye.
Tears nourish the dry riverbed.
My blue balloon has flown
to roam with the lost sea gull,
nowhere it belongs.

When I am forever gone,
come before my tomb,
bringing an Easter bunny
with my resurrected poems;
and in the desolate graveyard,
under the Plumeria fragrance,
my shadow will roam with you.

Two Solitudes

"Love consists of this: two solitudes that meet, protect
and greet each other." [54]
        – Rainer Maria Rilke

On the canvas of the night sky,
they often appear side by side,
sometimes further, sometimes nearer,
yet always at a distance
that they long to
but never cross.

Across the infinite time and space,
at one another they lovingly gaze,
communicating in silence
their unspoken words,
touching each other's soul
with their steadfast glow.

Two solitudes they remain,
roaming in the vast heavens,
with an invisible bond.
In darkness they shine
an eternal dream –
never to be fulfilled,
never to be shattered...

Angels dancing...

Have you watched angels dancing,
grass smiling, clouds dreaming,
stones weeping, love paining?

Have you heard the moon screaming,
stars whispering, flowers singing,
leaves moaning, ashes laughing?

Have you seen beauty in ugliness,
tenderness beneath coldness,
emptiness beside fullness,
sadness behind happiness,
strength from sorrowfulness,
despair in hope, hope in despair,
death in life, life in death?

O look up, down, around,
inside and the other side...

The Gaze

What unbreakable silence cries
in the unfathomable distance?
What impassable mountain lies
between soul and soul?
What impenetrable haze hides
the stars of true love?

Where may I find your tender gaze,
where may I turn my loving gaze,
when all around I feel and see,
silence below silence,
mountain after mountain,
haze before haze?

Rosy Dreams

The sun has set
but pink clouds still linger,
loathe to leave the blue canvas,
rosy dreams to cherish,
ephemeral, ethereal, extempore,
as if an angel had by chance left
some finishing touches of love.

No longer bright and passionate,
but a desperate tender pink
that makes a heart break .
Oh you love them the more
as in a moment they will be gone
when night curtains silently fall
and darkness descends
to enfold all.

Growing white

His hair snowy white,
her hair greyish white,
side by side they sit,
sharing a soft white ice-cream,
sweetly licking the drips,
soon to slip away.

Each thread of white holds
a memory of their story.
Each line of wrinkle traces
the long road they have walked,
how much bitterness they had to taste,
how many storms they had to brave,
before they could come close –

steadfast as two white barked trees,
sharing some sweetness at peace,
playing with the fading leaves,
watching the white snow fall,
embracing one world of white mist,
and together growing white?

To my piano

I fell in love with you
the first time my hands fell
on your keys, white and black.
You led me by and by
to drift and soar and fall
as melodies ebb and flow.
With your echoes my fingers dance,
love, pain, tears, joy, anger, sorrow,
sweeping across your mystic ocean.

Wave upon wave,
your music flows to me
along with memories and dreams,
intimately embracing my soul,
flying it across the gulf of time.
Flowers bloom, petals drop,
the last note holds and fades,
and somewhere lingers on...

The Violin

How it sobs
with each bow drawn
across the tightly strained
and soon to break strings
of its weeping heart in pain.

What sorrow trembles
in the depths of its soul?
What dream does it hopelessly dream
in the lonesome darkness,
never to be fulfilled?

How each sob
breaks my heart
into a thousand tears
falling into the ashes of flowers
that once so beautifully bloomed.

Does love come and go
like the music of a fleeting dream?
Never an easy piece to play
with the right touch and pace,
love is a song sprung
when the strings of two hearts
are taken by one starry bow.

Let my heart be touched
by the notes of love
and let it softly break
in the saddest song
of the sobbing violin...

To a distant cello

Your voice fell deep and low
into my waiting ears,
with the moan of the raindrops,
with the roar of the thunder,
knocking on my soul.

It doesn't matter
if you exist before my eyes
or just in my mind;
still I can intend you
through my act of emotion.

Your music ran,
magnetic and mellow,
across the meadow in my heart.
I heard the past, present and future,
carrying me away to a dream.

See you I cannot,
embrace you I cannot;
oh teach me please
where to suspend you –
out in the stormy air
or inside my restless heart?

Side by Side

"The purpose of relation is the relation itself, touching the
You. For as soon as we touch a You, we are touched by a
breath of eternal life." [55]
        – *Martin Buber*

Love wakens love;
heart touches heart.
Side by side they stay
upon the mirror of play
where shadows of clouds roam
and poems of leaves dance.

From some time ancient,
from some dream distant,
wind of eternity blows,
music of memory flows,
enfolding two souls.

If love is true,
if love is deep,
regardless of any distance,
it can wait in silence,
like the tenderness of water
in the depths of hearts.

Echoes of the rainbow

In the wind we meet;
in the wind we part.
Time will stretch very long,
like a lengthened rainbow,
from one end to the other.

A mulberry tree will grow,
a mad bird will sing;
and we shall wait
for the ripe fruits to fall,
the silkmoth to dance,
in the sweet echoes
of the magic rainbow.

Dancing with sorrow

"Dance beyond yourselves,
what does it matter if you've failed."[56]
       – Friedrich Nietzsche

You gave me a book
and a poem I wrote
upon a restless boat
of the sailing clouds,
longing to dance with love
into the eternal moon.

You gave me a pen
and a bridge I drew
across the ruthless waves
of the wide wild sea,
trying in vain to reach
the shoreline of a distant heart.

Let love drift, let love pain.
Still I love, still I write
hopeless hopes, fruitless fruits.
As words and bridges break,
let my music with sorrow dance
and may wounds enrich hearts.

A Solitary Path

"The poem is lonely and *en route*..." [57]
     – *Paul Celan*

If you come by this path –
you may see a leaf fall
and hear it whisper a name;
you may find a lily open
and remember a smile
that once bloomed for you;
you may overturn a stone
and find buried below
the fragments of some words
we once said and not said;
or you may remember nothing
hear nothing, find nothing,
only a lonely poem
drifting by a solitary path...

When life turns to dust

When life turns to dust
and the circle takes us back
to where we began,
when dead words rise
from ashes of death,
our souls will meet again –
roaming side by side
in the dionysian twilight,
rowing a mad boat
in the snow of the moon bed,
between death and non-death,
lost and not lost...

No longer

In the playground of life,
no longer will I cry
before any man's eyes
no matter how much pained.
I'd rather hold my head high,
watch men play, birds fly,
swings rise and fall,
feelings burn and die,
leaves and time drift by.

In the court of love,
no longer will I try
to argue the absurdity of fate,
plead for the mercy of love,
reason the fairness of treatment,
appeal against whatever punishment.
But tenderly I will give back
one heart for one heart,
two eyes for two eyes,
three kisses for each cold word,
four embraces for each sore hurt.

Dance in the fog

A broken poem,
bleeding, weeping,
drifting here, drifting there,
blindfolded by the mist,
trembling with tears and fears,
where's home? where's love?
in nightmares it screams,
failing to find its way.

Stay where you are,
an angel's voice says.
Explore and embrace –
mystery, sorrow, beauty…
When feet are too heavy,
spread wings wide,
dance, swing and swirl,
be grass swaying with nature's pulse,
be wind touching the shadowy fog,
rise and fall, slip and slide,
let soul guide…

清明- Ching Ming[58]

雨淚輕飄
春霧深鎖
讓一切愛恨, 哀愁, 遺憾
化成一片迷濛淒美
回憶披上白紗
變得模糊虛幻

靈魂在墓地徘徊
眼睛看不到眼睛
心尋找不到心
我是從墓穴飛來的蝴蝶
誤闖煩喧的凡塵
迷失在人世情網[59]

Rain tears lightly fall;
Spring fog deeply locks.
Let all sorrows, regrets, love, hate,
turn into a sea of beauty and haze.
Memories wear a white veil
become vague and unreal.

Souls linger in the graveyard.
Eyes fail to see eyes.
Hearts fail to find hearts.
A butterfly flies out from the tomb
wrongly enters this mundane world
and gets lost in the love web of men.

Diamonds and Rust

"We both know what memories can bring
They bring diamonds and rust." [60]
     – Joan Baez

Lightning of truth and untruth
strikes and cuts my mind,
tearing my thoughts to pieces
rolling across the unbridgeable gulf
between the past and present,
a comma and a full stop,
promises and ashes.

Under a beautiful naked tree
I sit with its fallen dreams,
clutching my weathered basket
of discoloured memories,
sorting out diamonds and rust
for which I had dearly paid
with the pearls of my heart,
with the tears of my moon...

A Barcarolle

When the pensive wind of winter blows,
when the music of the Barcarolle flows,
will you gaze at the sea of blue
and a boat of melody sail by,
rippling across the lake of your heart?

Perhaps souls will meet
in the music of old
in the horizon of haze
without bounds of time and space.

Lightly lightly drifts the boat;
softly softly it passes by
as the last note of ripple fades
to rise and dance again
in the echoes of memory…

A Solitary Song for Nothing

Remember the wind,
forget the wind,
playing the music of time and being.

Watch the sea gulls fly,
watch them meet and part,
over the ever-changing heart of sea.

Let me wander lonely as a poem,
drifting free between earth and sky;
dance with clouds of love and pain –
let me cry and smile,
and sing a solitary song for nothing.

Flowers like snow

"Only in the invisible innermost of the heart
is man inclined toward what is there for him to love." [61]
     – Martin Heidegger

If at long last you come
after all my endless winters,
when flowers start to dance
like snow in a hazy dream,
we'll seek the remnants of Spring
buried below the leaves of hope
that survive the cruelest frost
and the bitterest storm.

May sorrow melt
at the kiss of snow.
No more words we need
in this realm of pure.
Let snow petals fill
our empty bottles
and the invisible space
of our innermost heart.

A Solitary Song for Nothing
"The poem is lonely and *en route*..." [62]
– Paul Celan

I

In modern society dominated by finance, science and technology, poetry is something which very few people are interested in or care to read. Poetry is mostly considered as something impractical, nonproductive, obsolete, an escape from reality to the realm of dreams and fantasy, or at best a subject for the study of aesthetics and literature. Is the language of poetry remote, ambiguous, and of no relevance and value to the modern world of high tech and high speed? Is poetry just the expression of emotions or a kind of imitation or representation? Do poetry and philosophy have anything in common? Can poetry, like philosophy, offer some *Psycho-therapia* for our afflicted souls?

What have poets said about poems?
A poem should "be wordless as the flight of birds", "be motionless in time as the moon climbs", "be equal to: not true", "not mean but be".
(From *Ars Poetica*, Archibald MacLeish)

Poems are "paths on which language gets a voice, they are encounters, paths of a voice to a perceiving Thou... sketches of existence perhaps, a sending oneself ahead toward oneself, in search of oneself... A kind of homecoming."
(From *The Meridian*, Paul Celan)

"Poetry is the spontaneous overflow of powerful feelings: it takes its origin from emotion recollected in tranquility."
(From *Preface to Lyrical Ballads,* William Wordsworth)

"Poems are not...simply emotions...they are experiences. For the sake of a single poem, you must see many cities, many people and Things, you must understand animals, must feel how birds fly... You must be able to think back to streets in unknown neighborhoods, to unexpected encounters... You must have memories of many nights of love... And it is not yet enough to have memories. You must be able to forget them when they are many, and you must have the immense patience to wait until they return." (From Rainer Maria Rilke, *Letters to a Young Poet*.)

What have philosophers said about poetry?
In 'On the Division of the Fine Arts' Kant defines poetry as "the art of conducting a free play of the imagination as if it were a task of understanding"; words in poetry exceed the logic of concepts and the poet in playing "provides food for understanding and gives life to its concepts by means of his imagination".[63] To Kant, it is in the art of poetry that the power of aesthetic ideas can manifest itself to the full extent, aesthetic ideas meaning presentations of the imagination which prompt much thought but to which no determinate concept can be adequate, "the feeling of which quickens our cognitive powers and connects language, which otherwise would be mere letters, with spirit".[64]

Heidegger points out in, 'Poetically Man Dwells', that poetry is what really lets men dwell on this earth; poetry does not fly above the earth to escape it but is what first brings man onto the earth, makes him belong to it and brings him into dwelling.[65] Dwelling is "the manner in which mortals are on the earth"[66] and does not mean merely the occupying of a lodging. To Heidegger, poetic dwelling may counter the technological attitude towards an objectified nature or earth. In a destitute time[67] when God is dead and men are hardly aware and capable even of their own mortality but only exercise his assertive will to control nature and master the world, to be a poet means "to attend, singing, to the trace of the fugitive gods" and especially to gather in poetry the nature of poetry.[68] So what is the nature of poetry? I will try to explore below this nature in relation to truth, language and hermeneutics.

II
Truth

According to Heidegger, the nature of poetry is the founding of truth; and founding is understood as bestowing, grounding and beginning, and only actual in preserving.[69] Most people would think that poetry is just a matter of aesthetic consciousness for subjective pleasures to be derived therefrom. However poetry is more a disclosure of truth that it manifests within itself. The aesthetic consciousness is always secondary to the immediate truth-claim that proceeds from the work of an artist.[70]

Art, as the setting-into-work of truth, is poetry; the nature of art is poetry, as the letting happen of the advent of the truth of what is, and because of art's poetic nature, art breaks open an open place in which everything is other than usual.[71] The more purely the work is itself transported into the openness of beings opened by itself, the more simply it transports us out of the ordinary realm, and we submit to this displacement by transforming our accustomed ties to world and earth and restrain our usual doing and knowing to stay within the truth that is happening in the work.[72] Poetry helps us to see "the other side of things", illuminating another side of reality; it offers or creates an intimate or inner space issuing from the breakdown of ordinary familiarity with the real.

Truth is the truth of Being and beauty does not occur alongside and apart from this truth; the appearance of truth when it sets itself into a poem is beauty, which does not exist merely relative to pleasure and purely as its object.[73]

(a) Truth and untruth
   In 'On the Essence of Truth', Heidegger says that truth is not a feature of correct propositions asserted of an "object" by a human "subject" but the disclosure of beings through which an openness essentially unfolds".[74]
   Poetry is the creative preserving of truth in the poem and it is the becoming and happening of truth, which is the opening up of the Open[75] and the clearing of what is, and happens only as the openness is projected and sketched out.[76] When a poet composes a poem, truth happens as the clearing and concealing of what is. Poetry is not an aimless imagining of whimsicalities nor a flight of mere fancies into the realm of the unreal but an illuminating projection which unfolds of unconcealedness and projects ahead into the Open which poetry lets happen and in such a way that the Open brings beings to shine and ring out.[77] Truth is the unconcealedness of that which is as something that is, being the opposition of clearing and concealing, and happens only by establishing itself in the conflict and sphere opened up by truth itself.[78] According to Heidegger, "truth is un-truth, insofar as there belongs to it the reservoir of the not-yet-uncovered... in the sense of concealment."[79] The nature of truth of unconcealedness is dominated throughout by a denial, and truth in its nature is also untruth.[80] The truth of poetry is not governed by the distinction between true or false, and it is characteristic of the language of poetry that it speaks both truth and untruth and points to the open realm of interpretation.[81]

(b) Nearness

The truth of poetry consists in creating a "holding upon nearness", allowing us to experience nearness in such a way that this nearness is held in and through the linguistic form of the poem, and the poetic word brings the transience of time to a standstill and also "stands written" as a saying where its own presence is in play.[82]

According to Gadamer, the highest possibility of saying consists in catching its passing away and escaping and in making firm its nearness to being (a nearness not of this or that but of the possibility of everything); and what distinguishes the poetic word is its fulfilling itself within itself because it is a "holding of the near", summoning up what is "there" so that it is palpably near, and is not an empty word reduced to its merely signifying function.[83] The poetic word is able to capture and hold within itself this nearness and call a halt to what is fleeting; it has its enduring value in holding onto itself and in holding itself back, and in this it has its highest possibility.[84]

In this ever-changing world, poetry is where moments can be captured and memories forever stay. Poems preserve the concrete relations and sensations of the poet's experience, protesting against the transitory nature of such experience; they are the longing for and mourning of the unattainable as well as the accidental and analeptic glimpse into what is withheld.[85]

III
Language
(a) <u>Projective saying and Speaking purely</u>
To Heidegger, language is not only an audible and written expression of our communication but by naming beings for the first time, language first brings beings to word and to appearance and such saying is a projecting of the clearing, announcing what it is that beings come into the Open as; poetry is projective saying, the saying of the unconcealedness of what is, and language itself is poetry in the essential sense.[86] Language speaks and "what is spoken purely is the poem".[87] In writing poems, the poet does not use a word in the same way as ordinary speakers and writers do, but uses a word in an original way so that it becomes and remains truly a word.[88] Poetry does not take language as a material at its disposal but first makes language possible, and the essence of language should be understood as deriving from the essence of poetry.[89] Poetic language offers an alternative to the violence of technological rationality which defines, reduces, manipulates and exhausts its objects.[90]

(b) <u>Speculative and Opening up new possibilities</u>
According to Gadamer, language itself has something speculative about it as the realization of meaning and such realization is speculative in that the finite possibilities of the word are oriented toward the sense intended as toward the infinite; to say what one means and be understood means to hold what is said together with an infinity of what is not said in one unified meaning and ensure that it be understood in this way.[91] The poetic word is speculative not only as it requires a backdrop of the unsaid so that the explicitly said will also say what in the unsaid needs to come to be understood, it also has its own relation to being and brings something new into the realm of the said.[92] The poet frees himself of the ordinary and

customary words and usages and beholds the world as if for the first time and represents to us the new appearance of a new world in the imaginative medium of poetic invention; the suspension of the conventional patterns of being and thoughts enables the poet to hammer out new ways of thought and feeling.[93]

(c) Telling and New saying-power

What makes a word truly "a word" is that it stands and one stands by it; it is a telling word that speaks, that says something, and its being is comprised of as saying.[94] In poetry the true word comes forth, "the word as word speaks more tellingly than anywhere else" as it is not the dead letter of the writing but the resurrected word that can be assigned to the being of the work of art in poetry, and passage into writing brings to light the characteristically linguistic way-of-being of the word.[95] The forming of poetic language presupposes the dissolution of all conventionally accepted rules, which means that language is in the process of becoming and is not a rule-governed application of words, not a co-constructing of something in accordance with convention; the poetic word establishes meaning and the way it comes forth in a poem manifests a new saying-power.[96]

(d) Pure and Simple and Self-unfolding

Poetry is "the remembrance of language"; it wakens a secret life in words that had seemed to be used up and worn out, and tells us of ourselves.[97] The poetic word is self-standing, being irreducible to its signification. In ordinary discourse, we focus on what the discourse is conveying to us and let the appearance of the words disappear; but in poetry, the words are authentically there and come forth. Gadamer says that the distinguishing trait of the poetic word is its saying pure and simple and it stands as if before its own self-unfolding in the speech of the thinking word.[98] We tend to treat language as an object at our disposal and forget that language itself speaks. In a poem, language speaks, and such speaking is a telling in the highest degree; it is equally unfolding things and holding them back in readiness at the same time. Gadamer also considers that "poetry is language in the pre-eminent sense",[99] as it uses words in their highest possible valence[100] as words. Poetic language fulfills itself and not by confirmation sought through the verification of facts or further experience and thus "stands out as the highest fulfillment of that revealing which is the achievement of all speech".[101] Hence "the word finds its fulfillment in the poetic word – and from there enters into the thought of a thinking person."[102]

(e) Musicality, Sensuality and Ambiguity

In poetry one can experience the musicality and sensuality of language which exceeds categories of logic and concepts, meaning and contents of a subjective intention. Poetic language involves "a heterogeneity to meaning... resisting a singular and fixed meaning that would correspond to a subject's discrete intention".[103] The ambiguity of poetic language answers to the ambiguity of human life as a whole and therein lies its unique value.[104]

Poetic language has a kind of tone or musicality in itself. As Gadamer says, when one reads a poem, "it is as if the poem began to speak, as if it began to sing and one sings along with it".[105]

(e) Silence, limitation and danger

The real enigma of poetic language is "that in it the word not only stands out against the silent space around it but also bears traces of silence within itself."[106] How should one read the silence between the words as well as the resonance of silence within the word itself which loves to hide?

We should beware of the limitations and also the danger of language, its ability to lie and confuse and its threat to the loss of being. Language shows the paradox of saying what we realize cannot be said. "What is spoken is never, and in no language, what is said."[107]

As Heidegger remarks, "the word, once it is spoken, slips out of the protection of the caring poet, he alone cannot easily hold fast in all its truth the spoken knowledge of the reserving find and of the reserving nearness."[108]

IV
Hermeneutics

The word "Hermeneutics" comes from the Greek word *hermeneuein* ("to interpret") and the noun *hermeneia* ("interpretation"), which in turn are apparently derived from "Hermes", the wing-footed messenger-god, and is associated with the function of transforming what is beyond human understanding into a form that human intelligence can grasp.[109] In 'Holderlin and the essence of poetry', Heidegger says that the poet's saying is the intercepting of hints (the language of the gods) to pass them on to his people, which is both a receiving and new giving; it is new in the sense that the poet catches sight of what has been completed and boldly puts what he has seen into his words to foretell what is not yet fulfilled.[110] Heidegger considers a poet as an artist who "remains inconsequential as compared with the work, almost like a passageway that destroys itself in the creative process for the work to emerge."[111] We may see this not as a renunciation of the self by the poet, but rather a "transgression of the philosophical subject", that by "intuiting the ecstatic nature of the 'inner' self and the intimate nature of the external reality", the poet is brought into a heightened intimacy with the "other side of things".[112]

According to Heidegger, hermeneutics as a theory of understanding is a theory of ontological disclosure and language is a situation coming to explicitness in words; poetic speaking is a sharing of the world, a disclosure not of the speaker but of the being of the world.[113] When we read a poem, we should not treat it as a mere object of our subjectivity but an entity presenting itself as it is, as disclosing and manifesting itself to us in its own power of being. Hermeneutics has the deeper traditional overtones to bring out a hidden meaning, to reveal and disclose the unknown, to go behind the text to ask what the author did not and could not say but which comes to light therein as its innermost dynamic; truth is concealed as something which both emerges and plunges back into concealment, and interpretation must be open to the as yet unsaid.[114] Interpretation involves taking a back step from mere analysis and explanation to the achievement of thinking dialogue with what appears in the text, letting the language event happen; and understanding is not only a matter of questioning but a willingness to be open and learning how to wait and find the place out of which the being of the text will show itself.[115]

*

According to Gadamer, hermeneutics is the ontology and phenomenology of understanding which is a historical, dialectical, linguistic event; understanding is conceived not as an act of human subjectivity over and against an object but as the basic way of Dasein's being in the world.[116] Gadamer considers that the hermeneutical perspective is so comprehensive that it must even include the nature of beauty in nature and art.[117] This applies well to poetry, which is an object for hermeneutics, and hermeneutics operates especially in poetry. Poetry demands interpretation because of its inexhaustible ambiguity and cannot be satisfactorily translated in terms of conceptual knowledge; the poetic language is mythical as it requires no confirmation from anything beyond itself and the ambiguous meaning of poetry is bound up with the ambiguous meaning of the intentional word.[118] Language, being hermeneutical in its essence, is hermeneutical in the highest degree in poetry.[119] Compared with other art forms, the poetic artwork possesses as language a characteristic indeterminacy and the linguistic means at the disposal of poetry evoke presence, intuition and existence; in each person responding to the poetic word, that word is fulfilled in a unique intuitive fashion incommunicable to others.[120] This may be a kind of "subtle understanding" (妙悟) similar in a way to both Zen and poetry.[121]

*

Like other artworks, despite any temporal distance which may be present, good poems possess a contemporaneity that allows them to speak to us across the centuries with a special immediacy. A poem is the expression of a truth that cannot be reduced to what the poet actually thought and is open to a limitless array of ever new integrations; its real being is what it is able to say which goes beyond any historical confinement although a standard of appropriateness still applies amid such openness and richness of its possibilities for comprehension.[122] The language of a poem itself speaks and the reader's task is to understand and clarify the meaning of what it says which must be integrated into his or her self-understanding; hermeneutics bridges the distance between minds and reveals the foreignness of the other mind.[123] The experience of art is a task of integrating it into the whole of one's own orientation with the world and one's own self-understanding, and the language of art is constituted by the fact that it speaks to the self-understanding of every person as something ever present and through its own contemporaneity.[124]

*

Understanding a text (which may be a prose text or a poem) is like a conversation, and we make it speak by constructing the question of which the answer is in the text. As Gadamer says, part of real understanding is that we regain the concepts of a historical past in such a way that they also include our own comprehension of them; it is a fusion of horizons between the reader and the text.[125] The reader does not leave his own horizon behind but broadens it so as to fuse it with that of the text; the encounter with the horizon of the transmitted text lights up the horizon of the reader and leads to self-disclosure and self-understanding.[126] When a text speaks, it does not always speak its words the same in lifeless rigidity, but gives new answers to the person questioning it and poses new questions to the person answering it; and to understand a text is to come to understand oneself in a kind of dialogue and a text yields understanding only when what is said therein begins to find expression in the interpreter's own language.[127]

The key to understanding is not manipulation and control but participation and openness, not knowledge but experience, not methodology but dialectic.[128] The poet opens up, through his own openness to being, new possibilities in being, and to understand the poetic utterance designed to open up a new relationship to being, the interpreter must himself share something of the openness to new possibilities that the poet possessed.[129]

*

To understand a poem, we must first have a wish to understand it and let the words speak to us. Hermeneutics means not so much a procedure as a person's attitude who wants to understand someone else or a linguistic expression as a reader or listener.[130] We use our inner ear to hear what the words say.

We should also bear in mind that the presence of

real poetry always transcends the subjective horizon of interpretation of both the poet and interpreter. The singularity of the particular occasion can pass into a certain universality to make the poem accessible to everybody.[131] To Gadamer, the importance of the question "who am I and who are you?" is that it always remains open and such openness is renewed from poem to poem; what matters for Gadamer is not the identity of the "I" or "you" in the poems (that are pronounced in a shadowy-uncertain and constantly changing way) but the intimacy between them, an intimacy outside the determinacy of meaning and mediated by strangeness, and characterized by "the remoteness of the one nearest to us".[132]

We can see that a poem has its own existence detached from its creator. While outside information may help to protect against obvious error in interpretation and make understanding easier, it takes us only to the preliminary level and we should note that the same poem can be comprehensible with coherence and precision on a number of transpositional levels.[133] As Gadamer says, the poem does not bring to language a specific occurrence and readers can respond to what the language conjures up as if it were an offer and must supplement what they can perceive in a poem on the basis of their own experience, which "alone is what it means to understand a poem".[134] Readers incorporate the experience of the poem into the totality of their self understanding so that the poem really means something to them. The horizons of the readers' own world and self understanding are broadened; they become more fully present and do not leave home so much as they come home.[135]

*

We should bear in mind what Gadamer says: "All interpretation comes to share in the being of the poem"; poetry does not consist in intending something else but in the fact that what is intended and what is said is there in the poem and all interpretations offered are bound up with the existence of the poem and its ambiguous intimations.[136]

> *"Song, as you have taught it, is not a desire,*
> *not wooing any grace that can be achieved;*
> *song is existence...*
> *True singing is a different breath, that*
> *aims nowhere. A gust inside the god. A wind."*
> *– Rainer Maria Rilke,*
> *The Sonnets to Orpheus, First Part, III*

V
Poetry and Philosophy

According to Kant, aesthetic ideas are best expressed in poetry. Poetic language can give voice to what escapes the realm of legislative concept and rationality, like nature, joy, suffering, beauty and love which can be better expressed in poetic language than through philosophical concepts and rational truth-claims. Poetry can provide liberation for what is reduced to or forgotten by the language of concepts and reasons and free us from the limits and rationalism of philosophy. To Heidegger, poetic language is an access to truth, an entrance into thinking, and an alternative to the violence of technological rationality which manipulates and exhausts its objects.

We see that truth is what both poetry and philosophy is concerned about and share in common. Poetry can help us to gain insights into philosophical thoughts and draw us to the path of philosophy in search of truth, essence and meanings. Although philosophy may not provide us with definite answers, it "points the direction in which we have to search"[137] and "the very seeking is the goal and at the same time what is found."[138]

Poetry and philosophy can complement each other and give direction to thinking. While philosophy enriches poetry, giving it more depth and spirit, poetry brings philosophy closer to home and our heart, giving it a more personal, human and subtle touch so that it will not just seem to be a mass of hard concepts and dead words. Heidegger says poetry is the sister of philosophy. Poetry speaks to us in a more intimate tone while philosophy brings us to see things from a further distance and in a more objective and rational manner. We need the distance of philosophy, also the closeness of poetry.

Both poetry and philosophy can provide comfort to the diseased soul and help to drive out the affliction of the soul. Poetry like philosophy "is really homesickness, an urge to be at home everywhere", to be at once and at all times within the whole.[139] According to Heidegger, the original essence of joy is learning to become at home within a nearness to the origin, and the essence of nearness is that it brings near that which is near, yet keeping it at a distance.[140]

VI
The Encounter

A poem leads to an encounter linking what is apart. The poet Paul Celan says, "A poem, being an instance of language, hence essentially dialogue, may be a letter thrown out to sea with the – surely not always strong – hope that it may somehow wash up somewhere, perhaps on a shoreline of the heart. In this way, too, poems are on the way, they are headed toward."[141] So where is a poem heading toward? Will it ever reach the shoreline of the heart of an approachable other?

Celan also says, "The poem is lonely and *en route*... the poem intends another, needs this other...."[142] Its movement is not towards a point of being finished but a ceaseless, open-ended movement of indeterminacy towards what is always elsewhere, a pure exteriority: a freedom for which we have no words, a movement towards "the otherness" which it can reach and be free.[143]

A poem wants to reach the Other (thing or human being). It searches and addresses the Other; it becomes conversation. The poetic act is an act of thought which supposes intimacy or intimate difference, and to speak to the Other in the conversation is also a "letting speak", to prepare the presence of the Other within oneself, to let intimacy open up.[144] For Celan, "to write poems [is], so to speak, to orient myself, to find out where I was meant to go, to sketch out reality for myself."[145] Poems project existence and the poet lives in the direction in which it points. Self-understanding always occurs through understanding something other than the self, and the encounter with the Other is also a search of oneself, a homecoming.[146]

VII

We have seen from above the close relationship and significance of poetry to truth, language and hermeneutics. Although poetic utterance has something ambiguous about it, this is precisely where its hermeneutical truth lies.[147] Poetry, as the setting-into-work of truth, is a way to truth as well as to freedom. Though a lonely voice it sings in this world, it is a calling for man to turn towards the "innermost invisible region of the heart", for a transcendence that does not go up into something else but comes to its own self and the nature of its truth. Man is inclined towards what is there for him to love only in this inner and invisible region of the heart where he is free outside of the relation of the objects set around him and where rises the overflow of everything which is beyond the arithmetic of calculation and free of such boundaries into the unbounded whole of the Open; and "the widest orbit of beings becomes present in the heart's inner space".[148] Technology alienates us from nature and is opposed to the truth of poetic language as revealing disclosure. Men in the age of technology and commerce are absorbed in purposeful self-assertion and calculation and have parted from the Open, they need a conversion of consciousness or inner recalling to convert their nature which merely wills to impose into the innermost invisible region of the heart's space, and to convert the parting against the Open into an arriving at the widest orbit of the Open.[149] Poetry which is more fully saying is a song which is neither solicitation nor trade but existence itself, a song that does not cling to something eventually attained, "a breath for nothing". It is a solitary song whose voice is drowned in the modern world of technology and commerce where men strive to attain their objects and master the world.

*

A poem is an open-ended piece of work disclosing new possibilities in being, and should not be regarded as something that is simply aesthetic and lacking in existential seriousness. The experience of poetry is an experience of meaning brought about by understanding. The interpretation of a poem can bring about the self-interpretation of a reader who henceforth understands himself better or differently or begins to understand himself.[150]

*

We need poetry all the more in a sophisticated, commercialized and technical world where men will in the way of purposeful assertion of the objectifying of the world and building it up technologically thereby blocking their paths to the Open, where men have forgotten the true nature of dwelling and language and the relation of dominance between language and men gets inverted, where men have become the centre and measure of all things, with the sense of the sacredness of things being lost.

*

According to Heidegger, man is capable of poetry only to

the extent that his being is appropriate to that which itself has a liking for man and needs his presence, so long as kindness and the pure stay with his heart.[151] A poetized dwelling can help us find the way to the innermost space or home in our heart and enhance our understanding of ourselves and the world. The encounter with a poem is an event in which a world opens itself to us, letting new possibilities in being speak to us and address our understanding. While Heidegger emphasized the founding, grounding, dwelling and revealing nature of poetry and the renunciation of subjectivity, we should also bear in mind the play of imagination and intuition in poetry and the creativity and spontaneity of the poetic self, departing from absolute immanence to a transformed self and engendering a poetical experience of the world.[152] Poetry is truth and untruth, feeling and thought, imagination and experience, memory and hope, encounter and homecoming, creation and preservation, glimpse of life and mourning of loss, oscillating between love and pain, song and silence, freedom and nothing. Poetry brings us home to the innermost space of our heart where there is room for kindness and the pure, for poetic dwelling and imagination, for hope and love.

Patty Ho
June 2012

Notes on the CD accompanying the printed book.
Track contents, ISRC numbers and playing times.

Track No.	Track contents (Poem Title)	Language +	ISRC No. HK-D94-16-	Duration (mins)
1	Opening Announcement (in English)			4:30
2	Without Why	English	000001	2:28
3	Serenade	English	000002	1:32
4	Fragments	English	000003	2:00
5	Nocturne	English	000004	1:35
6	Miss you	English	000005	1:26
7	To part	English	000006	1:23
8	Will You?	English	000007	1:56
9	Maya	English	000008	2:29
10	A Rainy Lane	English	000009	1:57
11	Whispers in the waters	English	000010	1:39
12	A nostalgic zither 錦瑟	Chinese	000011	2:29
13	Flowerwords	Chinese/ English	000012	1:33
14	Boat of Sorrow許多愁	Chinese	000013	2:23
15	Flowers like snow	English	000014	1:57
16	The Voyage (A song never sung)	/	000015	1:58
17	Let's cry… let's smile	/	000016	2:28

18	Golden Shower	/	000017	1:32
19	Of walnuts and almonds / Of cakes and women	/	000018	2:08
20	Everything and Nothing	/	000019	1:41
21	Who?	/	000020	1:26
22	If you come...	/	000021	1:28
23	Pure and True	/	000022	2:03
24	Dancing with sorrow	/	000023	2:29
25	Two Solitudes	/	000024	2:00
26	Words	/	000025	1:45
27	Of leaves and ashes	/	000026	2:33
28	No longer	/	000027	1:33
29	清明- Ching Ming	/	000028	2:23
30	Side by Side	/	000029	1:58
31	The Gaze	/	000030	3:30
32	Final announcement (in English)			0.49

+ Language in which the poem is sung. (Please note that poems 16-30 inclusive have music but no songs.)

The music for all poems was composed by Patty Ho and arranged by Henry Poon. The following poems are sung by Patty Ho with Henry Poon at the piano: 'Without Why', 'Serenade', 'Fragments', 'Nocturne', 'Miss you', 'To part', 'Will You?', 'Maya', 'A Rainy Lane', 'Whispers in the waters', 'A nostalgic zither 錦瑟',

'Flowerwords', 'Boat of Sorrow許多愁', 'Flowers like snow', 'The Gaze'.

In Track No. 19, 'Of walnuts and almonds' and 'Of cakes and women' are dedicated to her father and mother respectively.

NOTE: Not all poems in the text appear also in the CD. Also, the sequence in which the poems as songs appear in the CD is different from the sequence in which the same poems appear in the book. The same is true of the poems in the CD which are accompanied by music only.

~~~~~~~~~~

PLEASE WRITE TO US!

We are interested to read your comments on
Patty Ho's
Of Leaves & Ashes.
Write to our email address, proverse@netvigator.com,
giving us a few sentences which you are willing for us to publish,
describing your response to this book.
If your comments are chosen to be included
in our E-Newsletter or website,
we will select another title published by Proverse
and send you a complimentary copy.
Please include your name, email address and mailing
address when you write to us, and state whether or not we
may cut or edit your comments for publication.
We will use your initials to attribute your comments.

Notes and Translations

¹ From the Preface in *The Peony Pavilion* (牡丹亭) by Tang Xianzu (湯顯祖):
情不知所起，一往而深，生者可以死，死者可以生。
None knows how love arises. It goes so deep that the living can die and the dead live again. (Translated by Patty Ho)

² From Book of Odes. Qin Feng. 'Reeds'《詩經‧秦風‧蒹葭》：
蒹葭蒼蒼，白露為霜。所謂伊人，在水一方。
溯洄從之，道阻且長。溯游從之，宛在水中央。
The reeds grow thick; the white dew turns to frost. The one whom I love is somewhere along the river.
I go upstream in search of her; the way is difficult and long.
I go downstream in search of her; she seems to be in the middle of the water. (Translated by Patty Ho)

³ *Milton on education: the tractate Of Education with supplementary extracts from other writings of Milton*, ed. Morley Oliver Ainsworth, New Haven, Yale UP, 1928, pp. 51-64, p. 60.

⁴ As can be seen from the many references and quotations of Rilke in this book.

⁵ WH Auden, 'Squares and Oblongs', in *Essays Based on the Modern Poetry Collection at the Lockwood Memorial Library, University of Buffalo*, by Karl Shapiro and others, 1st ed. New York: Harcourt, Brace [1948].

⁶ Quoted in, Marc Polonsky, 'Why Poetry', *The Poetry Reader's Toolkit: A Guide to Reading and Understanding Poetry*, Glencoe / McGraw-Hill, 2001, p. 5.

⁷ Martin Heidegger, 'Hölderlin and the essence of poetry' [the essay] in Werner Brock ed., *Existence and Being*. Chicago: A Gateway Edition, 1949, p. 271. The words

quoted above are used in the essay to explain why Hölderlin says that writing poems is "this most innocent of all occupations" and Heidegger points out that "by taking poetry as 'this most innocent of all occupations', we have not yet grasped its true nature". The rest of the essay unfolds this true nature and Heidegger says "poetry is a founding: a naming of being and of the essence of all things" and "poetry itself first makes language possible". Heidegger also says "poetry looks like a game and yet it is not", "what the poet says and undertakes to be is what is truly real", and "poetry is the most dangerous work and at the same time 'the most innocent of all occupations'".

[8] *Rainer Maria Rilke: Selected Poems*, translated by Albert Ernest Fleming, p. 160.

[9] As quoted in Martin Heidegger, *The Principle of Reason*, translated by Reginald Lilly, p. 36.

[10] From Empedocles, Fragments (Fragment. 26).

[11] From Heraclitus, Fragments (B-30).

[12] Martin Heidegger, *Being and Time*, translated by John Macquarrie and Edward Robinson, published in the *Harper Perennial Modern Thought series*, Harper Perennial Modern Classics, 2008, p. 63.

[13] Edmund Husserl, 'Philosophy as Rigorous Science' in *Phenomenology And The Crisis of Philosophy*, translated by Q. Lauer. New York: Harper & Row, 1965, p. 129.

[14] Hans-Georg Gadamer, 'On the contribution of poetry to the search for truth', in *The Relevance Of The Beautiful And Other Essays*, ed. Richard E. Palmer, Northwestern University Press, 2007, p. 115.

[15] "For all understanding remains partial and can never be terminated." From Wilhelm Dilthey, 'The Rise of Hermeneutics' in *The Hermeneutic Tradition : from Ast to Ricoeur*, ed. Gayle L. Ormiston and Alan D. Schrift.

Albany: State University of New York Press, c1990, p. 113.

[16] Jacques Derrida, "Différance". (Derrida published the famous essay 'Différance', which first appeared in the *Bulletin de la Société française de philosophie*, LXII, No.3 (July - September 1968), pp. 73-101. The essay was reprinted in *Théorie d'ensemble*, published by Editions Seuil in 1968.) "Différance" is a French term coined by Jacques Derrida, deliberately homophonous with the word "différence". "Différance" plays on the fact that the French word différer means both "to defer" and "to differ".

[17] Hans-Georg Gadamer, 'Language and Understanding', in *The Gadamer Reader: A Bouquet of the Later Writings*, Northwestern University Press, 2007, p. 107.

[18] From Heraclitus' Fragments (B-52).

[19] Edmund Husserl, *The Crisis of European Sciences and Transcendental Phenomenology*, translated by David Carr. Evanston: Northwestern University Press, 1970, p. 152.

[20] A Greek pre-Socratic philosopher, whose philosophy is best known for the cosmogenic theory of the four elements (earth, air, fire, water) and the powers of Love and Strife acting as forces to bring about the mixture and separation of the elements. According to the legend, he died by throwing himself into an active volcano, Mount Etna in Sicily.

[21] From the Fragments of Empedocles (Frag. 115) (*The Extant Fragments* by M.R. Wright, Yale University Press, 1981/Bristol Classical Press, 1995, pp. 155- 292. The numbering of the Fragments follows the arrangement of Diels-Kranz, *Fragmente der Vorsokratiker*.

[22] Hans-Georg Gadamer, 'Composition and Interpretation', in *The Relevance Of The Beautiful And*

Other Essays, translated by Nicholas Walker, Cambridge University Press, 1986, p. 71.

[23] 'The Sonnets to Orpheus', First Part, III, by Rainer Maria Rilke, *The Selected Poetry And Prose of Rainer Maria Rilke*, translated by Stephen Mitchell. New York: The Modern Library, 1995, p. 415.

[24] The painting, "苦瓜家園 (Home of Bitterness)", by Wu Guanzhong.

[25] "Sins are sins. Griefs are griefs. I am still I... Inevitable sins, bear them in peace; inescapable griefs, endure them in peace."
From a chapter in 勞思光《歷史之懲罰新編》(Lao Siguang, *The Punishment of History*, new ed., The Chinese University Press, 1999, p. 226.)

[26] *Rainer Maria Rilke: Selected Poems*, translated by Albert Ernest Fleming, p. 160.

[27] A reference to the ancient myth of Sisyphus.

[28] Rainer Maria Rilke, 'The Sonnets to Orpheus', First Part, III, *The Selected Poetry And Prose of Rainer Maria Rilke*, translated by Stephen Mitchell. New York: The Modern Library, 1995, p. 415.

[29] Friedrich Nietzsche, *Thus Spoke Zarathustra*.

[30] From 'Invitation to the Voyage' by Charles Baudelaire.

[31] In the painting《雙燕》'Two Swallows' by Wu Guanzhong.

[32] Holding a paper umbrella, alone
I walk hesitantly along the long, long
and lonesome rainy lane... (Dai Wangshu, 'Rainy Lane'. Translated by Patty Ho.)

[33] Friedrich Nietzsche, *Thus Spoke Zarathustra*.

[34] The beautiful zither without reason has fifty strings, each string, each post, recalling a splendid year.
Master Chuang was dazed by the butterfly in his dawn dream.

Emperor Wang entrusted to the cuckoo his heart of spring.
In the vast sea, below the bright moon, tears turned to
pearls.
In the Blue Fields, under the warm sun, jade gave off
smoke.
These feelings could wait to become memory,
but I felt too lost at that time.
(Li Shang Yin, 'Splendid Zither'.
Translated by Patty Ho.)
[35] Flowers not flowers, mist not mist,
coming in the midst of the night,
leaving at the break of dawn.
Like spring dreams they come for a while;
like morning clouds they go without trace.
('Bai Juyi, 'Flowers not Flowers'.
Translated by Patty Ho.)
[36] Wind subsides, dust scents, flowers have faded.
I feel too tired to comb my hair at dusk.
Things remain but not people; everything is over.
I want to speak, but tears first flow.
I have heard spring is still fair in Twin Brooks
and also intend to row a light boat,
but I fear the grasshopper boat there
can't move so much sorrow.
(Li Qingzhao, 'Spring of Wuling'.
Translated by Patty Ho.)
[37] Green green is your gown; long long is my love.
Even if I didn't go to you, couldn't you leave me some
words?
Green green is your pendant; long long are my thoughts.
Even if I didn't go to you, couldn't you come to me?
('Book of Odes. Zheng Feng. Lapel.'
Translated by Patty Ho.)
[38] Today last year in this door,

face and peach blossoms with each other shone red.
Don't know where face has gone;
peach blossoms still smile at the spring breeze.
(Cui Hu, 'Scribbling at a Village in the City South.'
Translated by Patty Ho.)
[39] Fallen flowers are not loveless;
they turn to spring soil and nourish flowers even more.
(Gong Zizhen, 'Miscellaneous Poem of ji-hai'.
Translated by Patty Ho.)
[40] Old friend comes to my dream,
knowing how I always miss him.
(Du Fu, 'Dreaming of Li Bai, two poems'.
Translated by Patty Ho.)
[41] Tang Wan唐琬, a poetess in the Southern Song
Dynasty, was married to the poet Lu You 陸遊who was
later forced by his mother to divorce the poetess.
[42] We go different ways; the present is no longer the past.
My sick spirit often sways like the ropes of a swing.
The horn sounds cold; the night is coming to an end.
Afraid of being questioned, I swallow my tears and make
up to look happy.
Hide! Hide! Hide!
(Tang Wan, 'The Phoenix Hairpin'.
Translated by Patty Ho.)
[43] Li Bai 李白, one of the greatest poets of the Tang
Dynasty.
[44] Abandoning me, yesterday could not be retained;
confusing me, today has got so many troubles.
…Take out the sword to break the water and more it
flows;
raise the cup to dispel sorrow and more sorrowful it feels.
Life in this world being so disappointing,
I'll loosen my hair and row a small boat next morning.

(Li Bai, 'Bidding Farewell to Secretary Shu Yun at Xie Tao Tower in Xuanzhou'. Translated by Patty Ho.)

[45] If life could stay just like the first meeting,
why would we lament for the fan in the autumn wind?
(Nalan Xingde, 'Mulan Hua: An Elegy'.
Translated by Patty Ho.)

[46] Men have sorrow, joy, parting and meeting,
The moon may be dim or bright, may wax or wane.
Such things have been imperfect since days of old.
May we live long and together share
this beautiful moon though far far apart.
(Su Shi, 'Water Song'. Translated by Patty Ho.)

[47] Not meeting each other,
we drift in life like the morning and evening stars.
What night is tonight
that we can gather in this candlelight?
(Du Fu, 'To my Retired Friend Wei'.
Translated by Patty Ho.)

[48] Spring dreams and autumn clouds,
Meeting and parting are so easy.
(Yan Jidao, 'Butterflies chasing flowers'.
Translated by Patty Ho.)

[49] At the far end of the front hills, blue clouds join;
in the clear night, there's a light sound of the white snow.
I wish to send my thoughts for you through the distant moon;
in the pale light of the lakeside, rain falls thick and fast.
(Du Mu, 'Sending to someone far away'.
Translated by Patty Ho.)

[50] *Paul Celan, Collected Prose*, translated by Rosmarie Waldrop. New York: The Sheep Meadow Press, 1986 [*Paul Celan, Collected Prose*], p. 49.

[51] English nursery rhyme and a popular children's song, often sung as a round. (*Wikipedia*)

[52] *Selected Poems And Prose of Paul Celan*, translated by John Felstiner. New York & London: W.W. Norton, 2001, p. 297.

[53] Ibid., p. 77.

[54] http://www.goodreads.com/quotes/7059-love-consists-of-this-two-solitudes-that-meet-protect-and

[55] http://www.myjewishlearning.com/article/i-and-thou-selected-passages/

[56] Friedrich Nietzsche, *Thus Spoke Zarathustra.*

[57] *Paul Celan, Collected Prose*, p. 49.

[58] A traditional festival usually in April when Chinese people visit the graves or burial grounds of their ancestors.

[59] Chinese poem by Patty Ho.

[60] From Joan Baez's lyrics for her song, 'Diamond and Rust'.

[61] 'What are Poets for', *op. cit.*, p. 125.

[62] *Paul Celan, Collected Prose*, p. 49.

[63] Immanuel Kant, *Critique of Judgment*, translated by Werner S. Pluhar, Hackett Publishing Company, 1987, p. 321.

[64] Ibid., 316.

[65] Martin Heidegger, 'Poetically Man Dwells', in Martin Heidegger, *Poetry, Language, Thought*, translated by Albert Hofstadter, Perennial Classics, 2001 [*Poetry, Language, Thought*], pp. 209-227, pp. 213, 216.

[66] 'Building Dwelling Thinking' in *Poetry, Language, Thought*, pp. 141-159, p. 146. Heidegger considers that human existence is poetic on its ground and "dwelling poetically" means both standing in the presence of gods and being struck by the essential nearness of things. See 'Hölderlin and the Essence of Poetry' in *Elucidations of Hölderlin's Poetry*, translated by Keith Hoeller. Amherst, N.Y. : Humanity Books, 2000, p. 60.

[67] Cf. Heidegger, "The time is destitute because it lacks the unconcealedness of the nature of pain, death and love". ('What are poets for?', in *Poetry, Language, Thought*, pp. 87-139, p. 95.)

[68] 'What are poets for?', in *Poetry, Language, Thought*, p. 92.

[69] 'The origin of the work of art', in *Poetry, Language, Thought*, pp. 15-86, p. 72.

[70] Hans-Georg Gadamer, *Philosophical Hermeneutics*, translated by David E. Linge, University of California Press, 1976), p. 5.

[71] 'The origin of the work of art', in *Poetry, Language, Thought*, pp. 72, 70.

[72] Ibid., p. 64.

[73] Ibid., p. 79.

[74] Martin Heidegger, *Basic Writings*, Harper Perennial Modern Thought, 2008, p. 127.

[75] Cf. Heidegger, "The Open is the great whole of all that is unbounded" in 'What are poets for?', in *Poetry, Language, Thought*, p. 104.

[76] 'The origin of the work of art', in *Poetry, Language, Thought*, p. 69.

[77] Ibid., p. 70.

[78] Ibid., pp. 79, 59.

[79] Ibid., p. 58.

[80] Ibid., p. 53.

[81] Hans-Georg Gadamer, 'Composition and Interpretation', in *The Relevance Of The Beautiful And Other Essays*, translated by Nicholas Walker, Cambridge University Press, 1986, [*The Relevance Of The Beautiful And Other Essays*], p. 73.

[82] 'Philosophy and poetry', in *The Relevance Of The Beautiful And Other Essays*, pp. 113-114.

[83] Hans-Georg Gadamer, 'On the truth of the word', in

The Gadamer Reader: A Bouquet of the Later Writings, edited by Richard E. Palmer, Cambridge University Press, 1986 [*The Gadamer Reader*], p. 153.

[84] Ibid., p. 155.

[85] Jennifer Anna Gosetti-Ferencei, *Heidegger, Hölderlin, and the Subject of Poetic Language*. Fordham University Press, 2004 [*Heidegger, Hölderlin, and the Subject of Poetic Language*], pp. 123, 129.

[86] 'The origin of the work of art', in *Poetry, Language, Thought*, pp. 71, 72.

[87] 'Language', in *Poetry, Language, Thought*, pp. 185-208, p. 192.

[88] 'The origin of the work of art', in *Poetry, Language, Thought*, p. 46.

[89] Martin Heidegger, 'Hölderlin and the Essence of Poetry', in *Elucidations of Hölderlin's Poetry*, translated by Keith Hoeller, Amherst, N.Y. : Humanity Books, 2000 [*Elucidations of Hölderlin's Poetry*], p. 60.

[90] *Heidegger, Hölderlin, and the Subject of Poetic Language*, p. 6.

[91] Hans-Georg Gadamer, *Truth And Method*, translated by Joel Weinsheimer & Donald G. Marshall, Second Revised Edition. New York: Continuum, 2004 [*Truth And Method*], p. 464.

[92] *Truth And Method*, p. 465; and Richard E. Palmer, *Hermeneutics Interpretation Theory in Schleiermacher, Dilthey, Heigedder, and Gadamer*, Evanston, Northwestern University Press, 1969 [*Palmer*], p. 211.

[93] *Truth And Method*, pp. 465, 466; and *Palmer*, p. 211.

[94] Hans-Georg Gadamer, 'On the truth of the word', in *The Gadamer Reader*, p. 137.

[95] 'On the truth of the word', in *The Gadamer Reader*, p. 143.

[96] Ibid., pp. 151, 152.

[97] *Truth And Method*, p. 446.

[98] 'On the truth of the word', in *The Gadamer Reader*, p. 153.

[99] 'On the contribution of poetry to the search for truth', in *The Relevance Of The Beautiful And Other Essays*, p. 106.

[100] See https://en.wikipedia.org/wiki/Valence

[101] Ibid., pp. 111, 112.

[102] 'On the truth of the word', in *The Gadamer Reader*, p. 155.

[103] Jennifer Anna Gosetti-Ferencei, *Heidegger, Hölderlin, and the Subject of Poetic Language*, Fordham University Press, 2004, p. 211.

[104] 'Composition and Interpretation', in *The Relevance Of The Beautiful And Other Essays*, p. 71.

[105] 'The Artwork in Word and Image', in *The Gadamer Reader*, p. 216.

[106] *Word Traces*, edited by Aris Fioretos, The Johns Hopkins University Press, 1994, p. 112.

[107] 'The thinker as poet', in *Poetry, Language, Thought*, pp. 1-14, p. 11.

[108] 'Homecoming/To Kindred Ones', in *Elucidations of Hölderlin's Poetry*, p. 49.

[109] *Palmer*, pp. 12, 13.

[110] 'Hölderlin and the Essence of Poetry', in *Elucidations of Hölderlin's Poetry*, p. 63.

[111] 'The origin of the work of art', in *Poetry, Language, Thought*, p. 39.

[112] *Heidegger, Hölderlin, and the Subject of Poetic Language*, pp. 128 , 240.

[113] *Palmer*, pp. 137, 139.

[114] *Palmer*, p. 147.

[115] *Palmer*, p. 155.

[116] *Palmer*, p. 215.

[117] 'Aesthetics and Hermeneutics', in *The Gadamer Reader*, pp. 124-125.

[118] 'Composition and Interpretation', in *The Relevance Of The Beautiful And Other Essays*, p. 69.

[119] *Palmer*, p. 155.

[120] Ibid., p. 70.

[121] 「大抵禪道在妙悟, 詩道亦在妙悟。」 (In general the way to Zen is subtle understanding and so is the way to poetry) quoted in 梁宗岱, 『談詩』 (Liang Zongdai, 'Poetry talk'), a chapter in 《詩與真》 (*Poetry and Truth*), Taiwan Commercial Press, 2002, p. 105.

[122] 'Aesthetics and Hermeneutics', in *The Gadamer Reader*, pp. 124-125.

[123] Ibid., p. 128.

[124] Ibid., p. 129.

[125] *Truth And Method*, p. 367.

[126] *Palmer*, p. 201.

[127] Hans-Georg Gadamer, *Philosophical Hermeneutics*, translated by David E. Linge, University of California Press, 1976, p. 57.

[128] *Palmer*, p. 215.

[129] *Palmer*, p. 211.

[130] Hans-Georg Gadamer, *Gadamer on Celan: 'Who am I and Who are You?' and other essays*, translated by Richard Heinemann and Bruce Krajewski, Albany, State University of New York Press, 1997 [*Gadamer on Celan*], p. 161.

[131] Ibid, p. 133.

[132] Ibid, pp. 26-28.

[133] Ibid, p. 133.

[134] Ibid., p. 134.

[135] *Palmer*, p. 168.

[136] 'Composition and Interpretation', in *The Relevance Of The Beautiful And Other Essays*, p. 72.

[137] Martin Heidegger, *The Fundamental Concepts of Metaphysics*, translated by William McNeill and Nicholas Walker. Bloomington: Indiana University Press, 1995, p. 4.

[138] Martin Heidegger, *Basic Questions of Philosophy*, p. 6.

[139] Martin Heidegger, *The Fundamental Concepts of Metaphysics*, translated by William McNeill and Nicholas Walker, Indiana University Press, 1995, p. 5.

[140] 'Homecoming/To Kindred Ones', in *Elucidations of Hölderlin's Poetry*, pp. 43-44.

[141] *Paul Celan, Collected Prose*, pp. 34, 35.

[142] Ibid, p. 49.

[143] *Gadamer on Celan*, pp. 19, 23.

[144] *Word Traces*, edited by Aris Fioretos, The Johns Hopkins University Press, 1994, pp. 148, 149.

[145] *Paul Celan, Selected Poems and Prose of Paul Celan*, translated by John Felstiner, W. W. Norton, 2001, p. 396.

[146] See Jennifer Anna Gosetti-Ferencei, 'A New Poetics Of Dasein', *Hyperion: on the Future of Aesthetics,* Contra Mundum Press Ltd, Vol. VIII, No.1 (2014), p. 15. "Poetic Dasein is never rid of alterity… and so the return home is never completed." "Dasein" is a term of Heidegger's, meaning "Being-there", a reference to human-beings in their existential condition.

[147] *Truth And Method*, p. 482.

[148] 'What are poets for?', in *Poetry, Language, Thought*, pp. 125, 128.

[149] Ibid, pp. 127, 128.

[150] Paul Ricoeur, 'What is a text? Explanation and Understanding', in *A Ricoeur Reader: Reflection and Imagination*, ed. by Mario J. Valdes, Toronto and Buffalo, University of Toronto Press, 1991, p. 57.

[151] 'Poetically Man Dwells', in *Poetry, Language, Thought*, p. 26.

152 *Heidegger, Hölderlin, and the Subject of Poetic Language*, pp. 241, 242, 251.

FIND OUT MORE ABOUT OUR AUTHORS
BOOKS AND EVENTS AND THE PROVERSE PRIZE

Visit our website
http://www.proversepublishing.com

Visit our distributor's website
<www.chineseupress.com>

Follow us on Twitter
Follow news and conversation: <twitter.com/Proversebooks>
OR
Copy and paste the following to your browser window and
follow the instructions: https://twitter.com/#!/ProverseBooks

"Like" us on www.facebook.com/ProversePress

Request our E-Newsletter
Send your request to info@proversepublishing.com.

Availability
Most titles are available in Hong Kong and world-wide
from our Hong Kong based Distributor,
The Chinese University Press of Hong Kong,
The Chinese University of Hong Kong, Shatin, NT,
Hong Kong SAR, China. Web: chineseupress.com

All titles are available from Proverse Hong Kong
and the Proverse Hong Kong UK-based Distributor.

We have stock-holding retailers in Hong Kong,
Singapore (Select Books),
Canada (Elizabeth Campbell Books),
Principality of Andorra (Llibreria La Puça, La Llibreria).

Orders can be made from bookshops in the UK and elsewhere.

Ebooks
Most of our titles are available also as Ebooks.

www.ingramcontent.com/pod-product-compliance
Lightning Source LLC
Chambersburg PA
CBHW062114080426
42734CB00012B/2861